I am praying
for continued
perseverance to
pursue the life God has for you!
Your future is bright and
sure stay the course!

Whoever would love life and see
good days must keep their tongue
from evil and their lips from deceitful
speech. They must turn from evil
and do good; they must seek
peace and pursue it.

I PETER 3:10–11 NIV

We don't drift in good directions.
We discipline and prioritize
ourselves there.

Andy Stanley

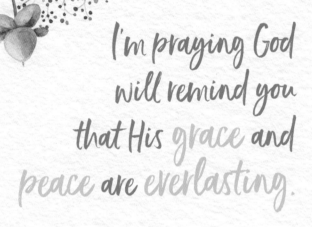

I'm praying God will remind you that His grace and peace are everlasting.

Therefore, since we have been justified through faith, we have peace with God through our Lord Jesus Christ.

ROMANS 5:1 NIV

Our righteousness doesn't depend on our present performance but on Jesus' finished performance.

Judah Smith

DaySpring

What is over our
head is at His feet.
I am praying you give
Him everything
the big and the small.
You are safe in His hands!

In peace I will lie down and sleep, for You alone,
LORD, make me dwell in safety.

PSALM 4:8 NIV

*Jesus wants you to lean on Him and hand over your burdens,
all of them. When you do, you'll experience a lightness of spirit
that knows no bounds.*

Charles Stanley

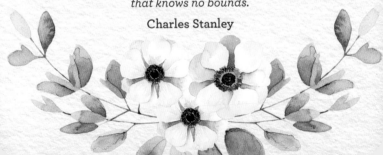

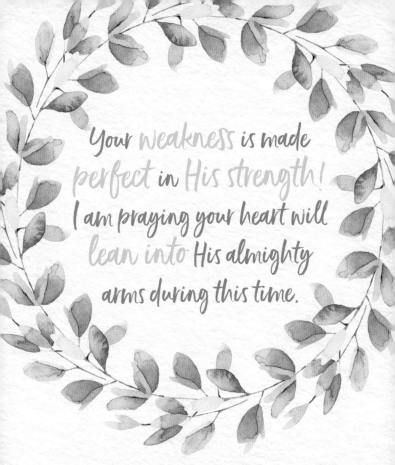

Your weakness is made
perfect in His strength!
I am praying your heart will
lean into His almighty
arms during this time.

Come to me, all who labor and are heavy laden, and I will give you
rest. Take my yoke upon you, and learn from me, for I am gentle
and lowly in heart, and you will find rest for your souls.
For my yoke is easy, and my burden is light.

MATTHEW 11:28–30 ESV

*Maybe wholeness is not reaching for perfection in your life;
maybe wholeness is embracing brokenness as part of your life.*

Ann Voskamp

DaySpring

I'm thanking
God for you today!
You bring peace to every
situation you encounter.
Thank you for being a
great role model for me.

Peacemakers who sow in peace reap
a harvest of righteousness.
JAMES 3:18 NIV

*When our souls are
healthy we change the
environment,
the environment
doesn't change us.*

Carl Lentz

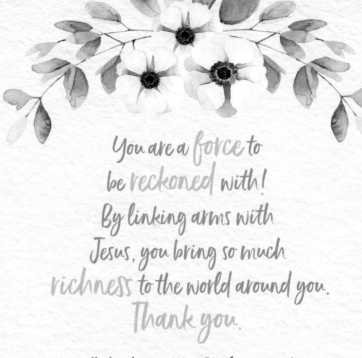

*You are a force to
be reckoned with!
By linking arms with
Jesus, you bring so much
richness to the world around you.
Thank you.*

Finally, brothers, rejoice. Aim for restoration,
comfort one another, agree with one another,
live in peace; and the God of love and peace will be with you.

II CORINTHIANS 13:11 ESV

We will never honor Christ if we forget to honor each other.

Bob Goff

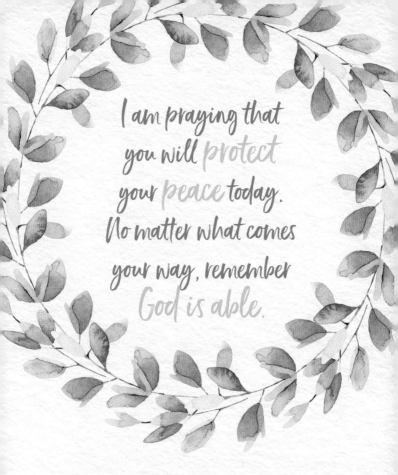

I am praying that
you will protect
your peace today.
No matter what comes
your way, remember
God is able.

Make every effort to keep the unity of the
Spirit through the bond of peace.

EPHESIANS 4:3 NIV

God will always speak peace and not confusion.
He will lead you, not drive you.

Roy Lessin

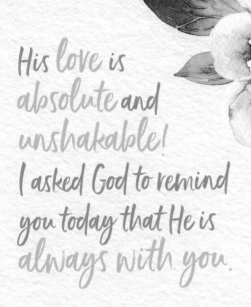

His love is absolute and unshakable! I asked God to remind you today that He is always with you.

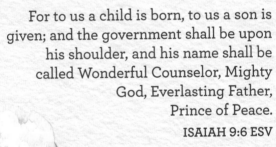

For to us a child is born, to us a son is given; and the government shall be upon his shoulder, and his name shall be called Wonderful Counselor, Mighty God, Everlasting Father, Prince of Peace.

ISAIAH 9:6 ESV

Peace: total well-being and security because God is with His people.

Sheila Walsh

I am praying you will be reminded of how truly loved you are by your Creator. He delights in you. Thank you for being a great role model for me.

For to set the mind on the flesh
is death, but to set the mind on
the Spirit is life and peace.

ROMANS 8:6 ESV

*Lord, make us
instruments of
Thy peace;
where there
is hatred.*

St. Francis of Assisi

Your life matters so much to Jesus!
I'm praying you'll see your
circumstances as an opportunity
to honor God with your story.

May God Himself, the God of peace, sanctify you
through and through. May your whole spirit,
soul and body be kept blameless at the
coming of our Lord Jesus Christ.

I THESSALONIANS 5:23 NIV

When love brings comfort, it is by God's compassion;
when love brings peace, it is by God's grace;
when love brings joy, it is by God's presence.

Bonnie Jensen

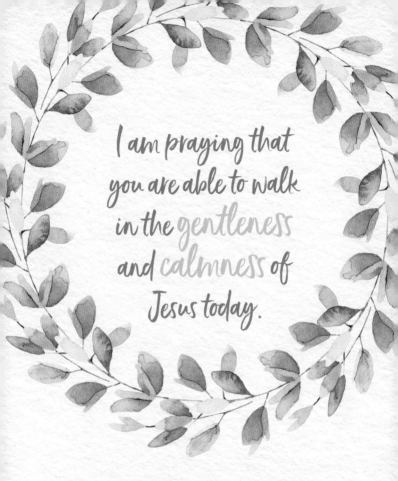

I am praying that you are able to walk in the gentleness and calmness of Jesus today.

Grace and peace to you from God our Father and the Lord Jesus Christ.

I CORINTHIANS 1:3 NIV

*When we appropriate God's great enablers—
His grace and His peace—we can achieve gentleness
and calmness even during hard times.*

Kay Arthur

I am praying
your trust and
confidence grow
today as you remember
He is for you.

But blessed is the one
who trusts in the LORD,
whose confidence is in Him.

JEREMIAH 17:7 NIV

*You will never need more
than He can supply.*

J. I. Packer

DaySpring

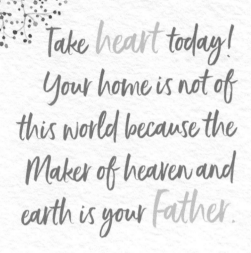

Take *heart* today!
Your home is not of
this world because the
Maker of heaven and
earth is your *Father*.

This is what the LORD says: Do not be afraid!
Don't be discouraged by this mighty army,
for the battle is not yours, but God's.

II CHRONICLES 20:15 NLT

*My home is in heaven.
I'm just traveling
through this world.*

Billy Graham

I pray you will find comfort in His goodness and peace today.

Agree with God, and be at peace; thereby good will come to you. Receive instruction from his mouth, and lay up his words in your heart.

JOB 22:21–22 ESV

The voice you believe will determine the future you experience.

Steven Furtick

DaySpring

I am praying you will breathe in the big life God has planned for you!

The Spirit of God has made me, and the breath of the Almighty gives me life.

JOB 33:4 ESV

God loves each of us as if there were only one of us.

Augustine

When you
follow Jesus,
you will not fail.
I am praying you are reminded
that He provides a peace that is
beyond understanding.

Great peace have those who love
Your law, and nothing can
make them stumble.

PSALM 119:165 NIV

*Let the consequences of your
obedience be left up to God.*

Oswald Chambers

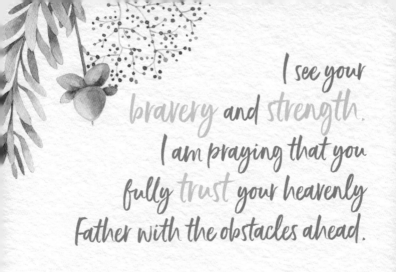

I see your bravery and strength. I am praying that you fully trust your heavenly Father with the obstacles ahead.

Be strong and courageous.
Do not fear or be in dread of them,
for it is the LORD your God who goes with you.
He will not leave you or forsake you.

DEUTERONOMY 31:6 ESV

*We are all faced
with a series of
great opportunities
brilliantly disguised as
impossible situations.*

Chuck Swindoll

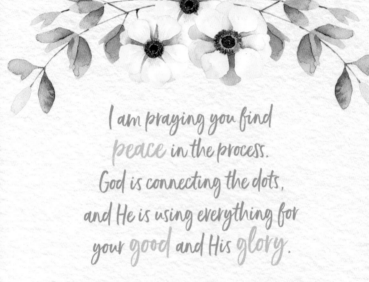

I am praying you find
peace in the process.
God is connecting the dots,
and He is using everything for
your *good* and His *glory*.

Therefore, my beloved brothers, be steadfast,
immovable, always abounding in the work of
the Lord, knowing that in the LORD
your labor is not in vain.

I CORINTHIANS 15:58 ESV

We are all rough drafts of the people we're still becoming.

Bob Goff

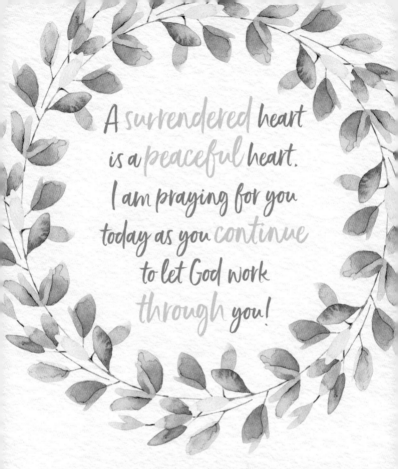

A surrendered heart
is a peaceful heart.
I am praying for you
today as you continue
to let God work
through you!

And we know that for those who love God all
things work together for good, for those who are
called according to his purpose.

ROMANS 8:28 ESV

Great people do not do great things;
God does great things through surrendered people.

Jennie Allen

I am praying
that your anxiety
about the future is replaced
with anticipation
about how God is at work.

Cast all your anxieties on Him,
because He cares for you.
I PETER 5:7 NIV

*You grow when your trust in
God exceeds your anxiety
about the future.*

Christine Caine

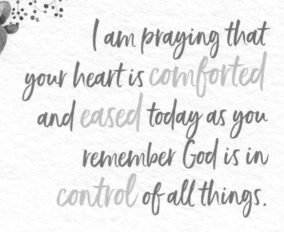

I am praying that your heart is comforted and eased today as you remember God is in control of all things.

For God is not a God of disorder but of peace, as in all the meetings of God's holy people.

I CORINTHIANS 14:33 NLT

We must settle in our hearts that no matter what, God is sovereign.

Beth Moore

Peace is yours! Praying you feel His presence close today.

Then He arose and rebuked the wind, and said to the sea, "Peace, be still!" And the wind ceased and there was a great calm.

MARK 4:39 NKJV

Peace doesn't come from finding a lake with no storms. It comes from having Jesus in the boat.

John Ortberg

I asked God to make you keenly aware of His presence today.

And having shod your feet with the preparation of the gospel of peace.
EPHESIANS 6:15 NKJV

Anywhere peace is lacking, the enemy is at work.
Priscilla Shirer

I am praying
you'll lean into
God for complete peace
in the midst of these
uncertainties and struggles.

Now the fruit of righteousness
is sown in peace by those
who make peace.

JAMES 3:18 NKJV

*Life with Jesus is not
immunity from difficulties,
but peace in difficulties.*

C. S. Lewis

DaySpring

You have a big, bright, beautiful future ahead of you! There is so much JOY on its way!

For length of days and long life and peace they will add to you.

PROVERBS 3:2 NKJV

Not only has your past been paid for, your future has been provided for.

Joyce Meyer

Radically loved.
Set apart.
Uniquely made.
You are God's masterpiece.

This is love: not that we loved God, but that
He loved us and sent His Son as an
atoning sacrifice for our sins.

I JOHN 4:10 NIV

Define yourself radically as one beloved by God.
This is the true self. Every other identity is illusion.

Brennan Manning

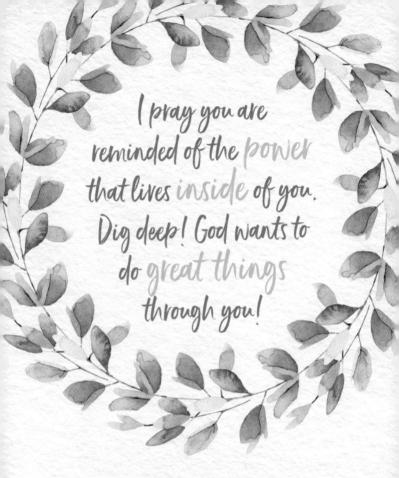

I pray you are reminded of the power that lives inside of you. Dig deep! God wants to do great things through you!

For the Kingdom of God is not just a lot of talk;
it is living by God's power.

I CORINTHIANS 4:20 NLT

*If we do the little things like they are big things,
then God will do the big things like they are little things.*

Mark Batterson

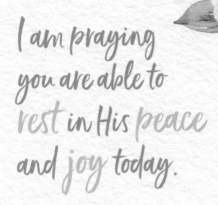

I am praying
you are able to
rest in His peace
and joy today.

For the things we see now will soon
be gone, but the things we cannot
see will last forever.

II CORINTHIANS 4:18 NLT

*Anything that undermines
your peace ultimately
undermines your happiness.*

Andy Stanley

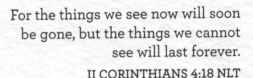

Your plans will be revealed in time! I'm praying God will show you more about who He is, and what He has planned for you.

I count everything as loss because of the surpassing worth of knowing Christ Jesus my Lord.

PHILIPPIANS 3:8 ESV

The Father doesn't give life directions in one big bundle because the goal is knowing Him, not the plan.

Louie Giglio

Praying you feel His
supernatural peace the kind
that the world can't give!

For what does it profit a man if he
gains the whole world and loses
or forfeits himself?

LUKE 9:25 ESV

*You're exhausted in the faith because you're looking at you.
The more you look at yourself and the less you look at God,
the more you get frustrated at yourself.*

Matt Chandler

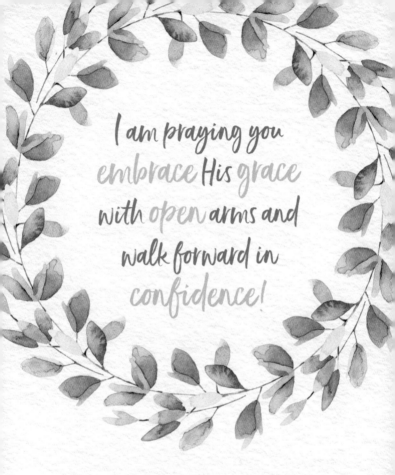

I am praying you
embrace His grace
with open arms and
walk forward in
confidence!

Therefore, if anyone is in Christ, the new creation
has come: The old has gone, the new is here.

II CORINTHIANS 5:17 NIV

*When you hold on to your history you do it
at the expense of your destiny.*

T. D. Jakes

I am praying
you'll be reminded
that the same God who
created the stars is the same
God who goes before you.

Is anything too hard for the Lord?
GENESIS 18:14 NIV

Everything you need
God already is.
Priscilla Shirer

Your best is ahead of you. Praying peace and joy will follow you today and always.

May the God of hope fill you with all joy and peace in believing, so that by the power of the Holy Spirit you may abound in hope.

ROMANS 15:13 ESV

Peace is the calm assurance that what God is doing is best.

James MacDonald

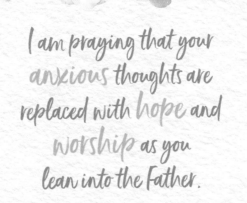

I am praying that your anxious thoughts are replaced with hope and worship as you lean into the Father.

And the God of all grace, who called you to His eternal glory in Christ, after you have suffered a little while, will Himself restore you and make you strong, firm and steadfast.

I PETER 5:10 NIV

When I understand that everything happening to me is to make me more Christ-like, it resolves a great deal of anxiety.

A. W. Tozer

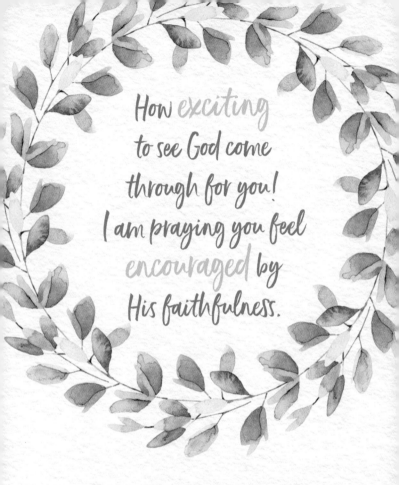

How exciting
to see God come
through for you!
I am praying you feel
encouraged by
His faithfulness.

Only fear the LORD and serve Him in truth with all your
heart; for consider what great things He has done for you.

I SAMUEL 12:24 NASB

I do not pray for success, I ask for faithfulness.

Mother Teresa

Just prayed
for you:
Remember, His peace
can break through anything.

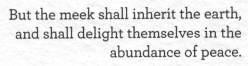

But the meek shall inherit the earth,
and shall delight themselves in the
abundance of peace.

PSALM 37:11 NKJV

*Right there where we
are most vulnerable,
the peace that is
not of this world is
mysteriously hidden.*

Henri Nouwen

Peace like a river.
Calm in the storm.
Rest amidst choas.
Praying you'll find
time to enjoy these
God-given gifts today.

The work of righteousness will be peace,
and the effect of righteousness,
quietness and assurance forever.

ISAIAH 32:17 NKJV

Ruthlessly eliminate
hurry from your life.

Dallas Willard

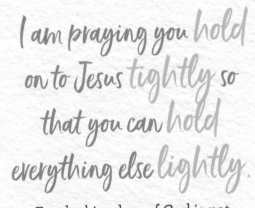

I am praying you hold on to Jesus tightly so that you can hold everything else lightly.

For the kingdom of God is not eating and drinking, but righteousness and peace and joy in the Holy Spirit.

ROMANS 14:17 NKJV

And so I urge you to enjoy this ministry of self-surrender. Don't push too hard. Hold this work lightly, joyfully.

Richard Foster

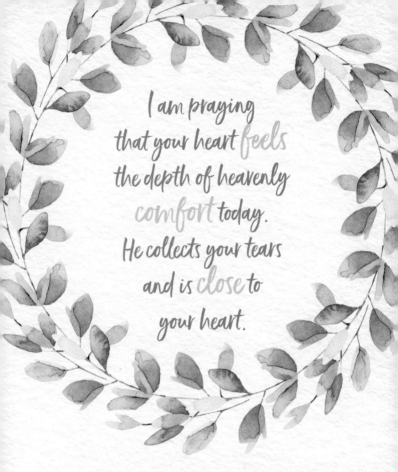

I am praying
that your heart feels
the depth of heavenly
comfort today.
He collects your tears
and is close to
your heart.

Blessed are those who mourn,
for they shall be comforted.

MATTHEW 5:4 ESV

I believe still today what I have always believed:
that God is good, that the world He made is extraordinary,
and that His comfort is like nothing else on earth.

Shauna Niequist

DaySpring

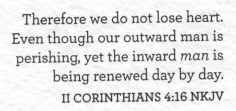

I am praying that you anchor yourself in God's love, deeply trusting that His ways are good.

Therefore we do not lose heart.
Even though our outward man is
perishing, yet the inward *man* is
being renewed day by day.

II CORINTHIANS 4:16 NKJV

*Faith is not opposed to
the mind. It's superior to
the mind which is why
the renewed mind
enhances faith.*

Bill Johnson

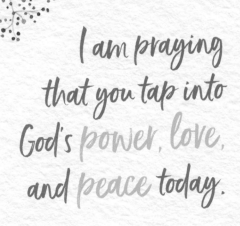

I am praying
that you tap into
God's power, love,
and peace today.

For God has not given us a spirit of fear,
but of power and of love and of a sound mind.
II TIMOTHY 1:7 NKJV

*We need no wings to go in
search of Him, but have
only to look upon Him
present within us.*

St. Teresa of Avila

Praying
you'll find true
peace of mind today.

The LORD will give strength to His people;
the LORD will bless His people with peace.

PSALM 29:11 NIV

A mind at peace, beautifies the plainest
surroundings and even in the hardest conditions.

J. R. Miller

I am praying
for you as you
follow Jesus.
Let Him be
your guide.

The Lord is my shepherd, I lack nothing.
He makes me lie down in green pastures,
He leads me beside quiet waters

PSALM 23:1–2 NIV

There are no experts in the company of Jesus.
We are all beginners, necessarily followers,
because we don't know where we are going.

Eugene Peterson

Problems will always exist, but peace is always within reach. Praying you'll be reminded of who is in control.

The LORD *is* good, a stronghold in the day of trouble; and He knows those who trust in Him.

NAHUM 1:7 NKJV

Peace is within reach, not for lack of problems, but because of the presence of a sovereign Lord.

Max Lucado

DaySpring

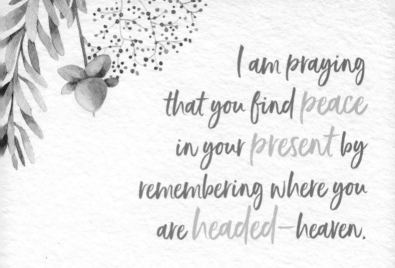

I am praying
that you find peace
in your present by
remembering where you
are headed—heaven.

Above all, you must live as citizens of
heaven, conducting yourselves in a manner
worthy of the Good News about Christ.

PHILIPPIANS 1:27 NLT

Inner peace doesn't
come from getting what
we want, but from
remembering
who we are.

Marianne Williamson

I'm praying you'll
be filled with
God's peace today.

Cast your burden on the LORD, and he will sustain
you; he will never permit the righteous to be moved.

PSALM 55:22 ESV

How powerful prayer is!
May we never lose the courage to say:
Lord, give us Your peace.

Pope Francis

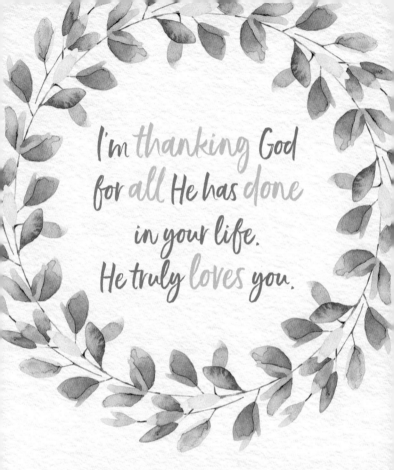

I'm thanking God
for all He has done
in your life.
He truly loves you.

O Lord, I will honor and praise Your name, for You are my
God. You do such wonderful things! You planned them long
ago, and now You have accomplished them.

ISAIAH 25:1 NLT

*Concentrate on counting your blessings and
you'll have little time to count anything else.*

Woodrow Kroll

The power
that lies within
you is mighty!
Praying you feel
empowered today.

For the word of the cross is folly to those
who are perishing, but to us who are
being saved it is the power of God.

I CORINTHIANS 1:18 ESV

*No God, no peace;
know God, know peace.*

Croft M. Pentz

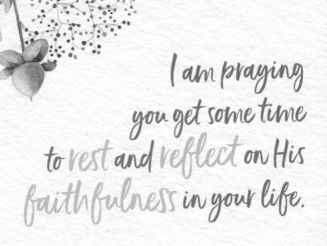

I am praying you get some time to rest and reflect on His faithfulness in your life.

Return to your rest, my soul,
for the LORD has been good to you.

PSALM 116:7 NIV

Sabbath is a circuit breaker for idolatry.

Andy Crouch

*Joy is yours in Jesus!
Praying you are able
to soak it up today!*

Joyful are people of integrity, who follow the
instructions of the LORD. Joyful are those who obey
His laws and search for Him with all their hearts.

PSALM 119:1–2 NLT

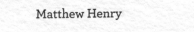

Holy joy will be oil to the wheels of our obedience.

Matthew Henry

DaySpring

Praying you feel His strength as you continue forward!

Many are the plans in a person's heart,
but it is the LORD's purpose that prevails.

PROVERBS 19:21 NIV

*How you live your life is a testimony
of what you believe about God.*

Henry Blackaby

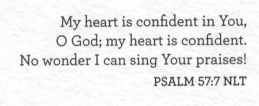

I am praying
for you and what
is next for your life.
I know He will give you
confidence for the next step.

My heart is confident in You,
O God; my heart is confident.
No wonder I can sing Your praises!

PSALM 57:7 NLT

*He knows we need
dreams in pieces
because we would
be too scared of
the whole puzzle.*

Annie Downs

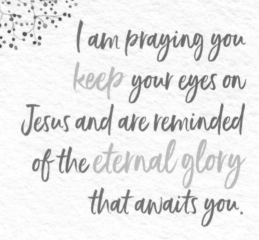

I am praying you keep your eyes on Jesus and are reminded of the eternal glory that awaits you.

For I consider that the sufferings of this present time are not worth comparing with the glory that is to be revealed to us.

ROMANS 8:18 ESV

Look within,
get depressed;
Look around,
get distressed;
Look to Jesus,
find perfect rest.

Joseph Prince

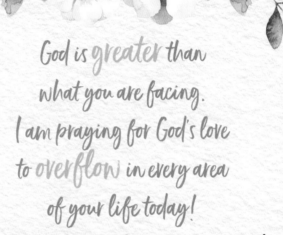

*God is greater than
what you are facing.
I am praying for God's love
to overflow in every area
of your life today!*

For the sake of Christ, then, I am content with
weaknesses, insults, hardships, persecutions,
and calamities. For when I am weak, then I am strong.

II CORINTHIANS 12:10 ESV

There is no pit so deep that God's love is not deeper still.

Corrie ten Boom

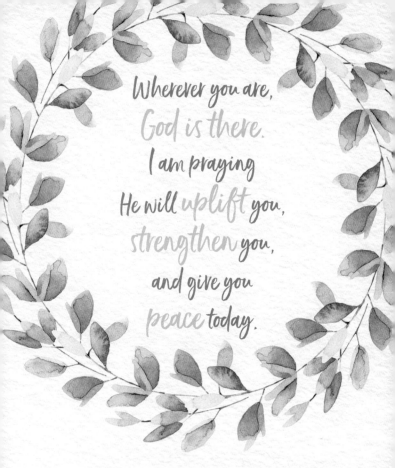

Wherever you are,
God is there.
I am praying
He will uplift you,
strengthen you,
and give you
peace today.

Continue steadfastly in prayer,
being watchful in it with thanksgiving.
COLOSSIANS 4:2 ESV

*There is a vast difference between talking about
God and listening to a God who talks to you.*

Lisa Bevere

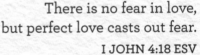

Praying
you feel His
comfort today.

There is no fear in love,
but perfect love casts out fear.

I JOHN 4:18 ESV

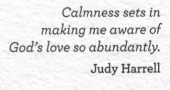

*Calmness sets in
making me aware of
God's love so abundantly.*

Judy Harrell

Praying God will
shine His bright
light on you today.

Again Jesus spoke to them, saying,
"I am the light of the world.
Whoever follows me will not walk
in darkness, but will have the light of life."

JOHN 8:12 ESV

*Never doubt God in the
darkness what He has
given us in the light.*

Francine Rivers

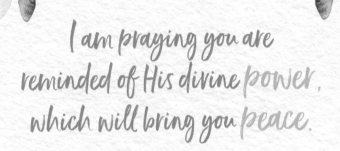

I am praying you are reminded of His divine power, which will bring you peace.

I know that all God does will last forever;
there is no adding to it or taking from it.
God works so that people will be in awe of Him.
ECCLESIASTES 3:14 HCSB

Awe is a sense for the transcendence, for the reference everywhere to Him who is beyond all things.
Abraham Joshua Heschel

DaySpring

Praying you
sense Him
close today.

Draw near to God,
and he will draw near to you.
JAMES 4:8 ESV

*What makes life splendid is
the constant awareness of God.*

Albert Edward Day

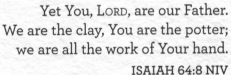

Praying God will whisper words of peace to your heart today.

Yet You, LORD, are our Father.
We are the clay, You are the potter;
we are all the work of Your hand.

ISAIAH 64:8 NIV

*The still, small voice is
never silent. No matter
where you are, no matter
what you're dealing with,
if you sit for a moment in the
stillness of His presence,
His voice will come to
you—quietly—and whisper
words of peace.*

Triest Van Wyngarden

Rest is always possible with Jesus. Always. I asked God to remind you to breathe today.

Let us, therefore, make every effort to enter that rest, so that no one will perish by following their example of disobedience.

HEBREWS 4:11 NIV

For our growth in power and happiness depends upon the number of seconds out of each twenty-four hours that we are resting in God.

Glenn Clark

I am praying He will
show you just how much of
a difference you are making
in the lives of those around you.

He must increase,
but I must decrease.
JOHN 3:30 ESV

I want to preach the
Gospel with my life.
Charles de Foucauld

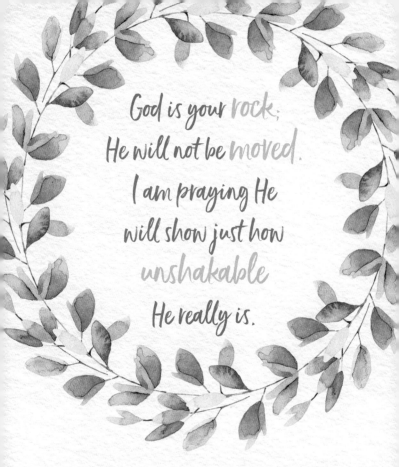

God is your rock;
He will not be moved.
I am praying He
will show just how
unshakable
He really is.

There is no one holy like the LORD, indeed, there is
no one besides You, nor is there any rock like our God.

I SAMUEL 2:2 NASB

Is the peace of God in the soul disturbed by things down here?
No, never! If waters break in stormy currents against a rock,
the rock is unmoved; it is only the waters that are disturbed.

G. V. Wigram

Praying you
are surrounded
by His peace no matter
what the world brings your way.

He is not afraid of bad news; his heart is
firm, trusting in the LORD.

PSALM 112:7 ESV

*Jesus calls us to surrender and
there's nothing like releasing
fears and falling into peace.
It terrifies, true. But it exhilarates.
This, this is what I've always
wanted and never knew: this
utter trust, this enlivening fall of
surrender into the safe hands.*

Ann Voskamp

DaySpring

Keep dreaming big!
Praying that you feel
strengthened as you walk
in radical obedience to
the faithful King.

If you abide in me, and my words abide
in you, ask whatever you wish,
and it will be done for you.
JOHN 15:7 ESV

*Be outrageous
enough to trust God.
Don't be adjusting
your vision downward.
Keep believing for
radical things
in Christ.*

Brian Houston

Run your race and
keep your eyes fixed ahead.
I pray you persevere, find courage,
and continue onward.

Let your eyes look directly ahead and let your gaze be
fixed straight in front of you. Watch the path of your
feet and all your ways will be established.

PROVERBS 4:25–26 NASB

*Peace is not merely a distant goal that we seek,
but a means by which we arrive at that goal.*

Martin Luther King Jr.

DaySpring

I am asking God to give you *hope, joy,* and *peace* during this time.

The LORD will bless His people with peace.

PSALM 29:11 KJV

Where Jesus is, we see Light in the darkest places . . .
Hope in times of uncertainty . . .
Joy in difficult circumstances . . .
Peace in the midst of activity . . .
Compassion in the presence of need!

Anonymous

I'm sorry that
life has felt like
one big rainstorm lately.
I'm praying He helps you see
life from His point of view.

Blessed is the man who remains steadfast
under trial, for when he has stood the
test he will receive the crown of life,
which God has promised to
those who love him.

JAMES 1:12 ESV

*When you accept the fact that
sometimes seasons are dry and
times are hard and that God is in
control of both, you will discover a
sense of divine refuge, because the
hope then is in God and not in yourself.*

Charles Swindoll

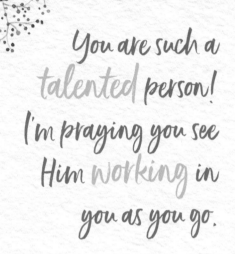

You are such a talented person! I'm praying you see Him working in you as you go.

God is able to make all grace abound to you, so that having all sufficiency in all things at all times, you may abound in every good work.
II CORINTHIANS 9:8 ESV

Fear is a manipulative emotion that can trick us into living a boring life.

Donald Miller

I am praying His
unfailing love covers you
like a tidal wave today.

Whoever pursues righteousnessness and unfailing
love will find life, righteousness, and honor.

PROVERBS 21:21 NLT

Our ultimate aim in life is not to be healthy,
wealthy, prosperous, or problem free.
Our ultimate aim in life is to bring glory to God.

Anne Graham Lotz

I am praying God
will take away all
your worries and
replace them with
thoughts of His love.

Physical training is good, but training for godliness is much
better, promising benefits in this life and in the life to come.

I TIMOTHY 4:8 NLT

*You are either becoming more like Christ every day or you are
becoming less like Him. There is no neutral position in the Lord.*

Stormie Omartian

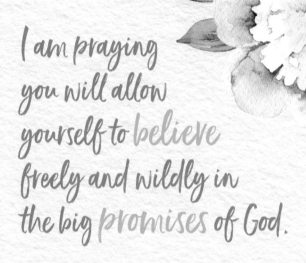

I am praying you will allow yourself to believe freely and wildly in the big promises of God.

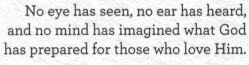

No eye has seen, no ear has heard, and no mind has imagined what God has prepared for those who love Him.

I CORINTHIANS 2:9 NLT

In God's plan,
there are no ends . . .
only corners that turn us
toward the next path of our lives.

Holley Gerth

I am praying you'll trust that He has given you everything you need to walk in peace and live joyfully.

For where your treasure is,
there your heart will be also.
MATTHEW 6:21 NIV

Whatever sits on the other side of your "if-only" is where you are looking for life, peace, joy, hope, and lasting contentment of heart.

Paul David Tripp

DaySpring

I am praying for
your day today that you
let His wisdom guide your
life and direct your steps.

But the wisdom from above is first pure, then
peaceable, gentle, open to reason, full of mercy and
good fruits, impartial and sincere.

JAMES 3:17 ESV

If the Almighty directs our steps,
we've no need to look back over our shoulders.

Liz Curtis Higgs

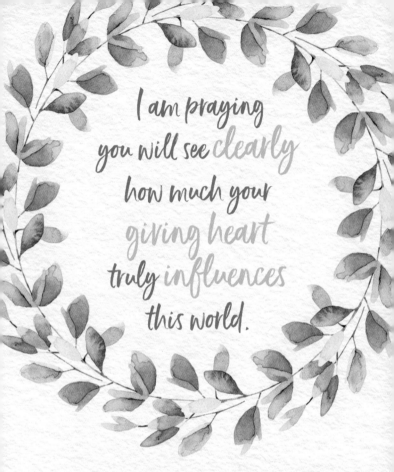

I am praying
you will see clearly
how much your
giving heart
truly influences
this world.

But whoever would be great among you must be your servant,
and whoever would be first among you must be slave of all.

MARK 10:43–44 ESV

*If you want to feel alive and if you want to feel
peace and happiness, give your life away.
Do something that is outside of
yourself for someone else.*

Natalie Grant

In surrendering
our life to Him,
we learn what it
means to truly live.
I am praying you are encouraged
by how much your life shines
the light of Jesus.

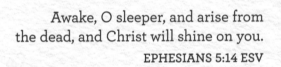

Awake, O sleeper, and arise from
the dead, and Christ will shine on you.

EPHESIANS 5:14 ESV

The truth is,
once you learn
how to die,
you learn how to live.

Mitch Albom

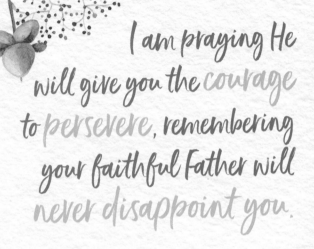

I am praying He will give you the courage to persevere, remembering your faithful Father will never disappoint you.

Let us hold fast the confession of
our hope without wavering,
for he who promised is faithful.
HEBREWS 10:23 ESV

*Don't be afraid to step
out and trust God.
He is more faithful than
the rising of the sun.*

Kari Jobe

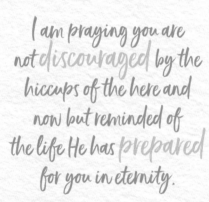

I am praying you are
not discouraged by the
hiccups of the here and
now but reminded of
the life He has prepared
for you in eternity.

So flee youthful passions and pursue righteousness,
faith, love, and peace, along with those who call on
the Lord from a pure heart.

II TIMOTHY 2:22 ESV

Peace convicts, forgives, and delivers you.
Peace will finish His work in you.
Peace will welcome you into glory

Paul David Tripp

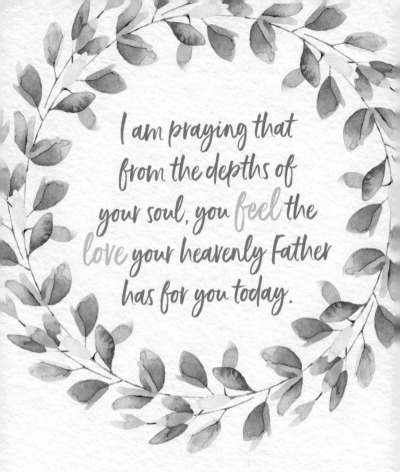

I am praying that
from the depths of
your soul, you feel the
love your heavenly Father
has for you today.

For he satisfies the longing soul,
and the hungry soul he fills with good things.

PSALM 107:9 ESV

*Look for yourself, and you will find in the long run only hatred,
loneliness, despair, rage, ruin, and decay. But look for Christ and
you will find Him, and with Him, everything else thrown in.*

C. S. Lewis

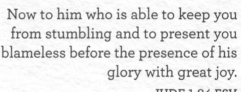

I am praying
you see yourself
the way your Savior
sees you blameless and
sure so that you can walk
forward in confidence.

Now to him who is able to keep you
from stumbling and to present you
blameless before the presence of his
glory with great joy.

JUDE 1:24 ESV

The waters are rising,
but so am I.
I am not going under,
but over.

Catherine Booth

The goodness of God is like an ever-flowing, unstoppable river. I pray you feel His presence and delight in His goodness today.

Praise be to the Lord, to God our Savior,
who daily bears our burdens.

PSALM 68:19 NIV

*Once we are
assured that
God is good,
then there
can be nothing
left to fear.*

Hannah Whitall Smith

DaySpring

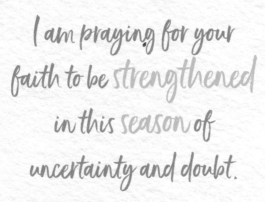

I am praying for your faith to be strengthened in this season of uncertainty and doubt.

The apostles said to the LORD, "Increase our faith!"

LUKE 17:5 NIV

The best thing to do with the best things in life is to give them up.

Dorothy Day

I am praying God
shows you that
He is right by
your side today.

My sheep hear My voice,
and I know them, and they follow Me.

JOHN 10:27 KJV

Trust—it's like a muscle. We were meant to grow stronger.
Gripping, struggling...and then knowing we must let go.
And when the wrestling stops, His peace overwhelms.

Cleere Cherry

I am praying
God will take all
the bricks out of
your bookbag so you can
travel lightly today.

Anxiety weighs down the heart,
but a kind word cheers it up.

PROVERBS 12:25 NIV

God has no
problems,
only plans.
There is never
panic in heaven.

Corrie ten Boom

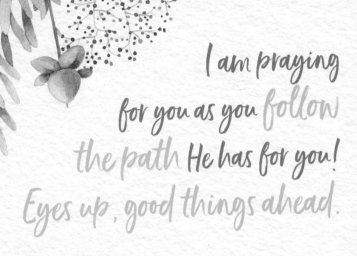

I am praying for you as you follow the path He has for you! Eyes up, good things ahead.

Follow the life-map absolutely, keep an eye out for the signposts, His course for life set out in the revelation to Moses; then you'll get on well in whatever you do and wherever you go.

I KINGS 2:3 THE MESSAGE

How happy we are when we realize that He is responsible, that He goes before, that goodness and mercy shall follow us.

Lettie Cowman

Praying His strong hand is your guide today.

Pursue the things over which Christ presides.
Don't shuffle along, eyes to the ground, absorbed
with the things right in front of you.

COLOSSIANS 3:1 THE MESSAGE

*He that loves works out good to those
that he loves, as he is able. God's power and
will are equal; what He wills He works.*

John Owen

I am praying
you will trust
God and His great
plans for you.

For the word of the LORD holds true,
and we can trust everything He does.

PSALM 33:4 NLT

The riddles of God are more satisfying
than the solutions of man.

G. K. Chesterton

DaySpring

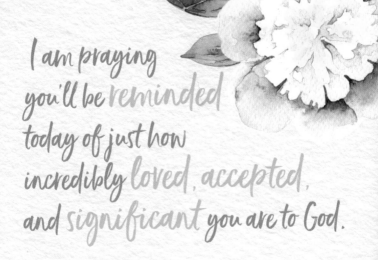

I am praying you'll be reminded today of just how incredibly loved, accepted, and significant you are to God.

However, I consider my life worth nothing to me; my only aim is to finish the race and complete the task of testifying the good news of God's grace.

ACTS 20:24 NIV

We are more loved and accepted in Jesus Christ than we ever dared hope.

Tim Keller

DaySpring

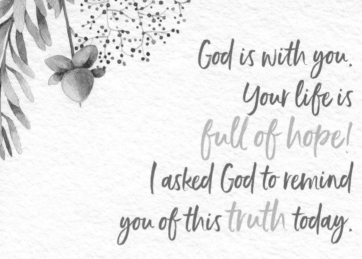

God is with you.
Your life is
full of hope!
I asked God to remind
you of this truth today.

No one will be able to stand against you as long as you live. For I will be with you as I was with Moses. I will not fail you or abandon you.

JOSHUA 1:5 NLT

We should ask God to increase our hope when it is small, awaken it when it is dormant, confirm it when it is wavering, strengthen it when it is weak, and raise it up when it is overthrown.

John Calvin